D0840181

This book belongs to:

Made in the USA
Columbia, SC
12 July 2023

20377016R00111